MW00986178

(wordless diagrams)

(wordless diagrams)

NIGEL
HOLMES

BLOOMSBURY

Published by Bloomsbury Publishing, New York and London
Distributed to the trade by Holtzbrinck Publishers

All papers used by Bloomsbury Publishing are natural, recyclable products
made from wood grown in well-managed forests. The manufacturing
processes conform to the environmental regulations of the country of origin.

Library of Congress Cataloging-in-Publication Data has been applied for.

ISBN 1-58234-522-8
ISBN-13 9781582345222

First U.S. Edition 2005

10 9 8 7 6 5 4 3 2 1

Printed in China by C&C Offset Printing Co. Ltd.

To Erin

ACKNOWLEDGMENTS

A huge thank you to Caroline Herter, whose idea this was in the first place, and who made it happen. Many and heartfelt thanks to Erin McKenna for research, general advice, and friendly but firm criticism. Among others who have helped and commented on the diagrams are Cidele Curo, and Robin and Ed Poska.

A few of these drawings first appeared in different forms (and usually with words). These are the art directors who kindly invited me to work with them on those early versions: Richard Aloisio, Bob Ciano, Steve Hoffman, Holly Holliday, Mirko Ilic, Christian Kuypers, Bambi Nicklen, Robert Priest, Mitch Shostak, Joe Ward.

INSPIRATION

Gerd Arntz, Harry Beck, Walter Bernard,
Henry Dreyfuss, David Driver, Brian Haynes,
Della van Heyst, Hazel Holmes, Rowland Holmes,
Paul Mijksenaar, Thelonious Monk, Jo Mora,
Eadweard Muybridge, Otto Neurath,
Bruce Robertson, Richard Saul Wurman

ⓘⓃⒹⒺⓍ

*Dangerous! Don't try this at home, even if you have your own tiger. The publisher and artist take no responsibility for damaged heads, helmets, or beach balls.

MORE INDEX!

*The record set on July 4th, 2004, by Takeru Kobayashi
in the International Federation of Competitive Eating contest
held at Coney Island, New York.

1

2

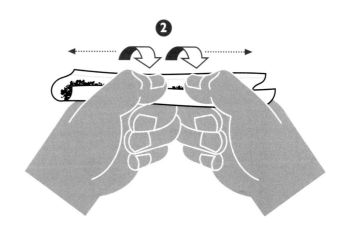

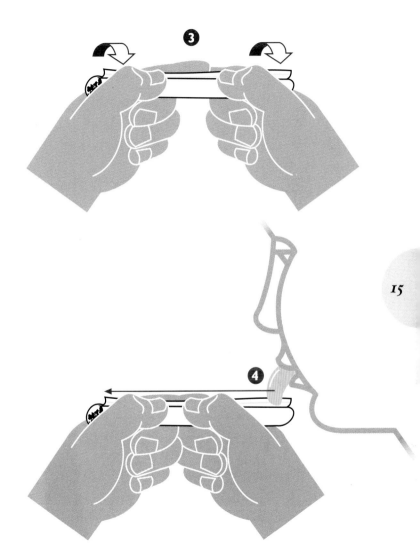

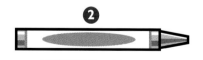

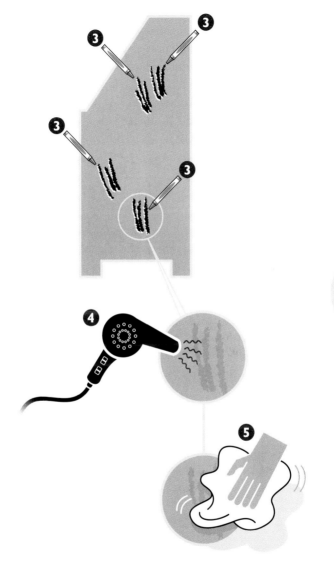

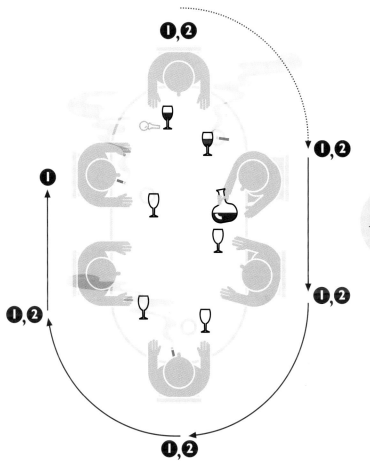

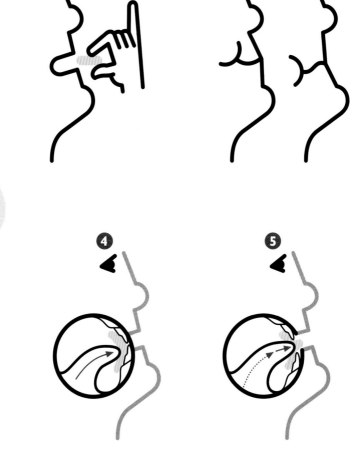

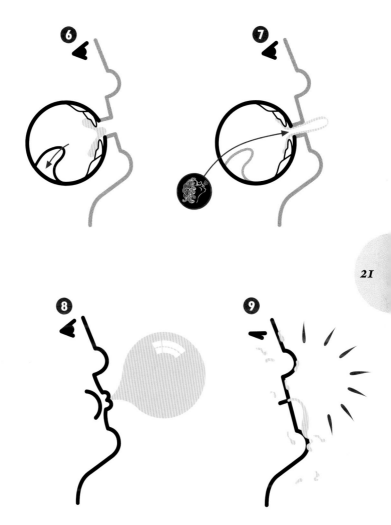

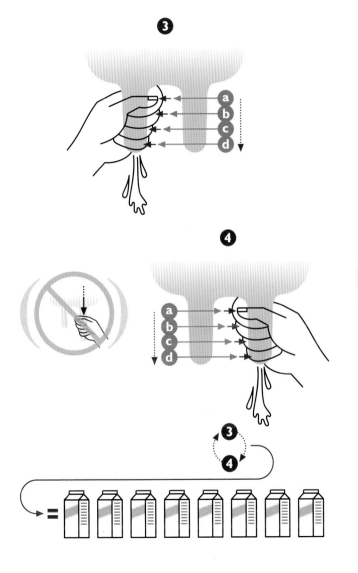

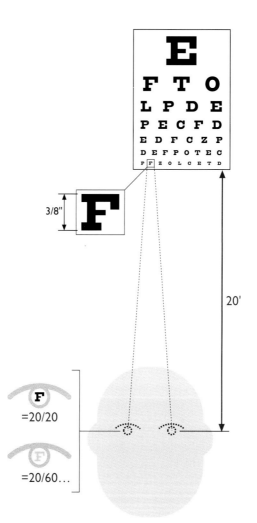

E

F T O

L P D E

P E C F D

E D F C Z P

D E F P O T E C

P F Z O L C E T D

F
3/8"

F
=20/20

F
=20/60...

20'

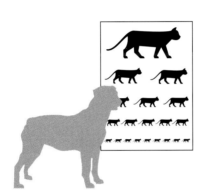

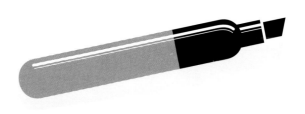

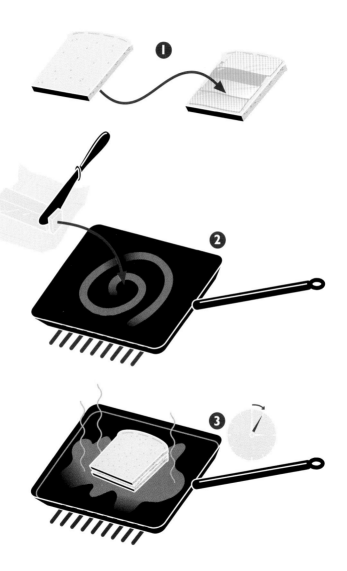

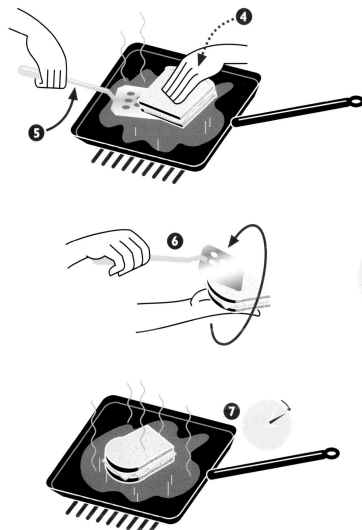

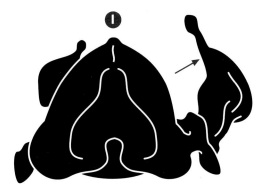

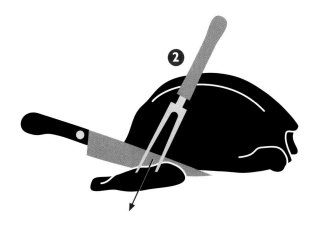

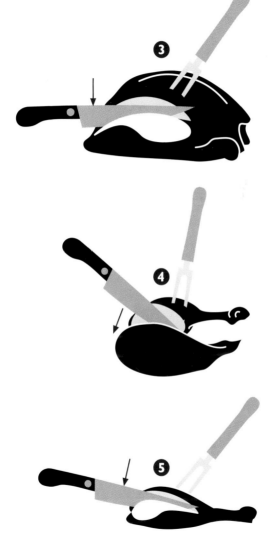

34

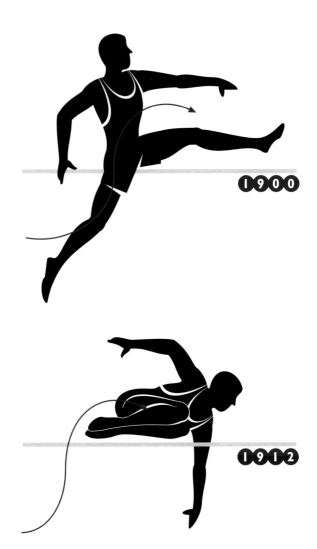

1900

1912

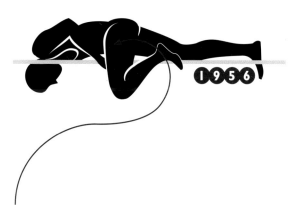

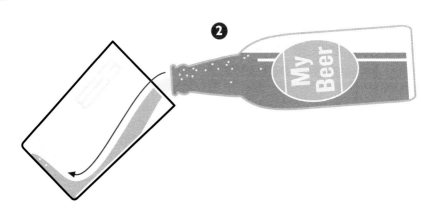

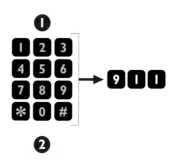

40

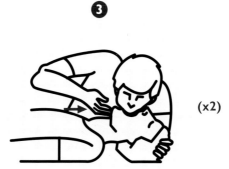

(x2)

4

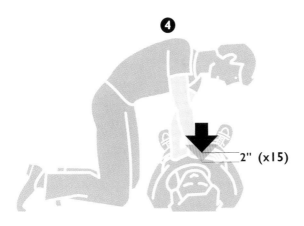

2" (×15)

5

(×2)

6

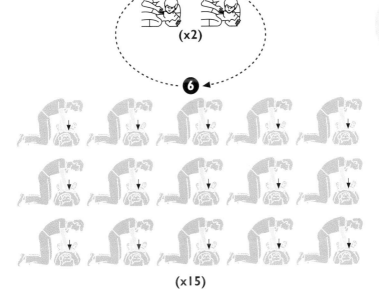

(×15)

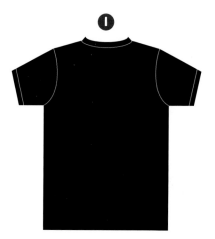

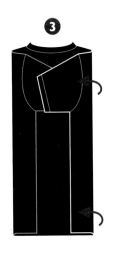

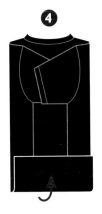

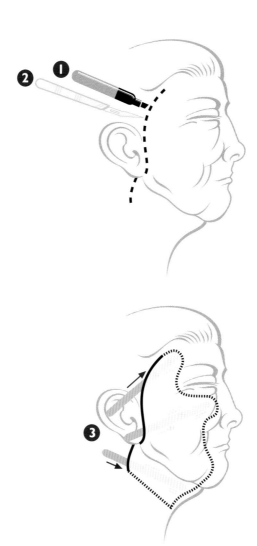

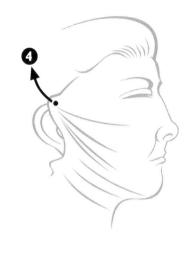

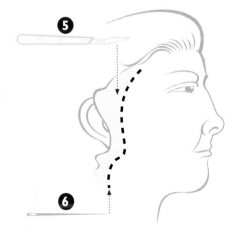

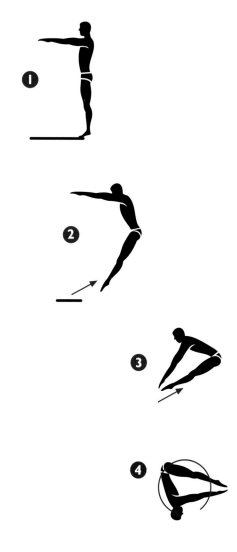

5

6

49

7

8

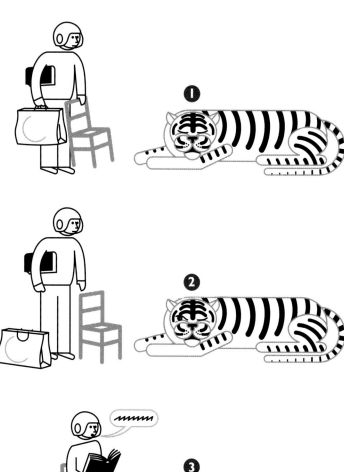

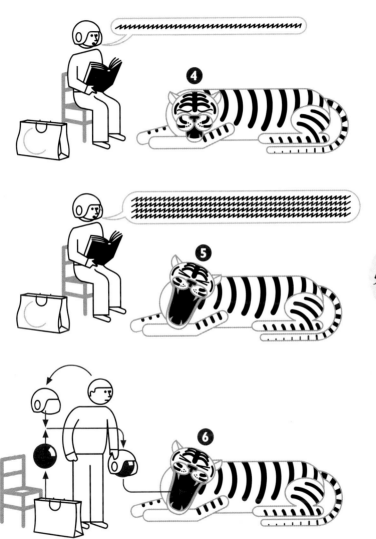

53

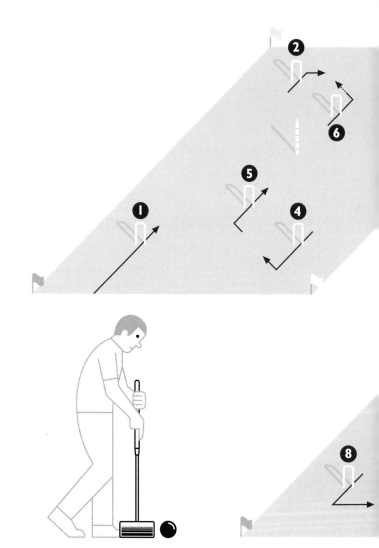

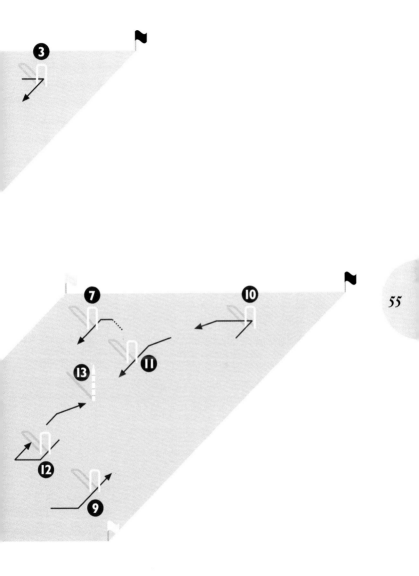

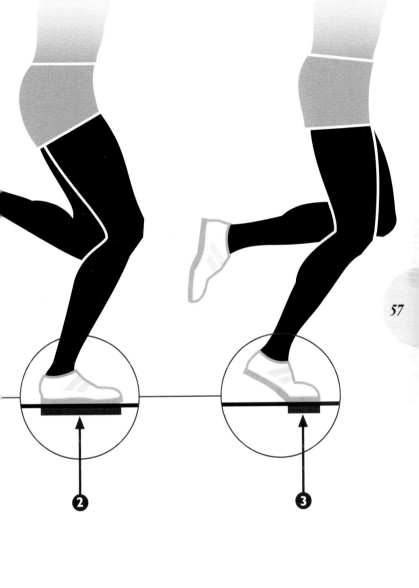

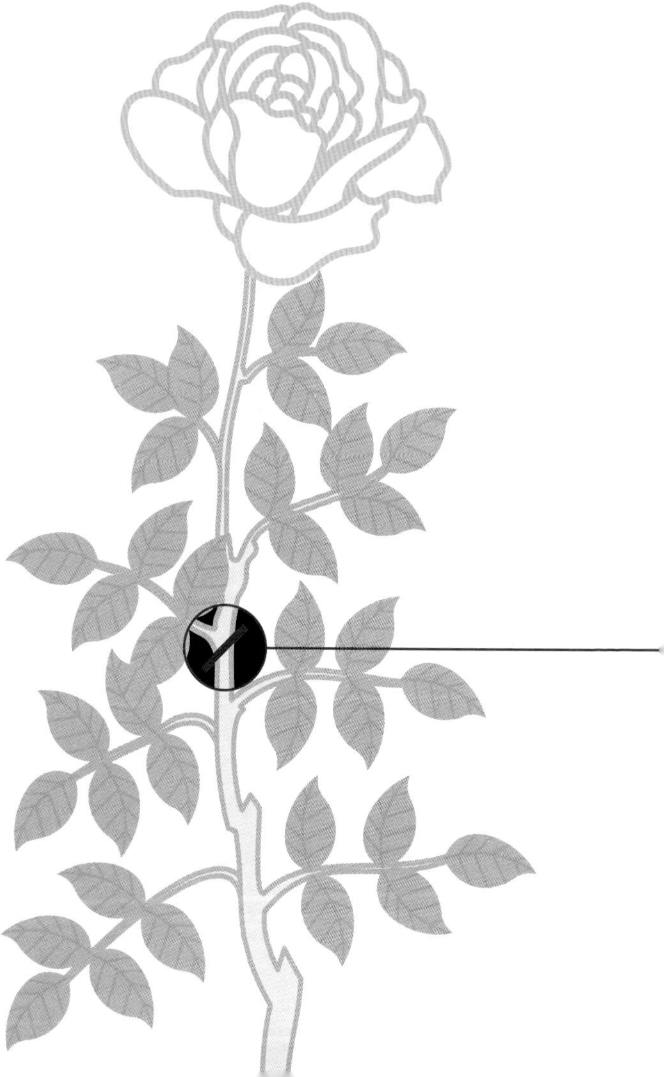

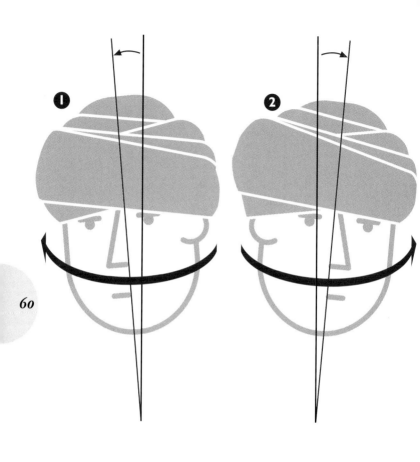

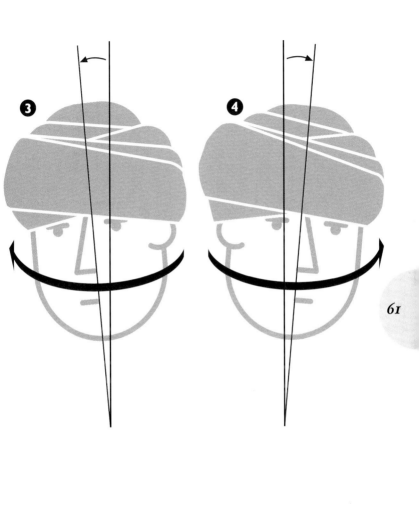

❸

❹

61

❶　**❷**

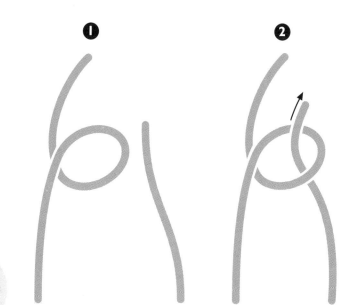

3 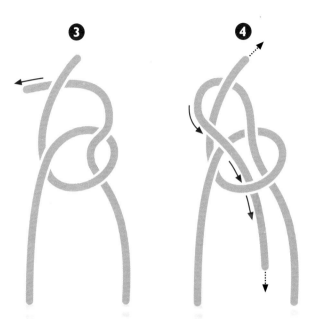 **4**

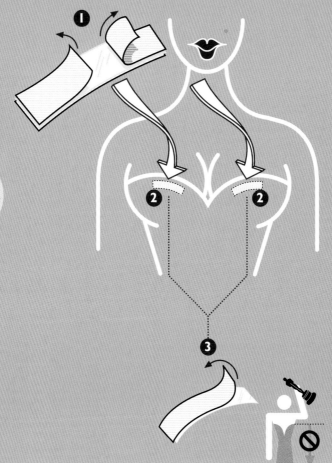

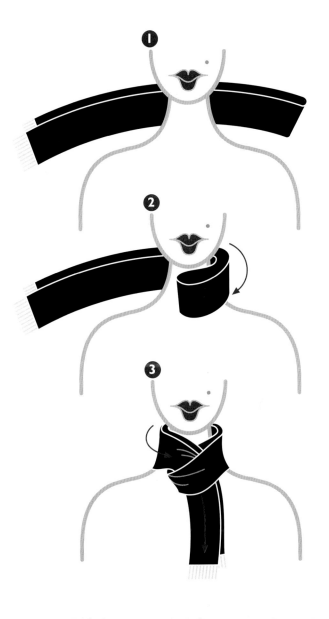

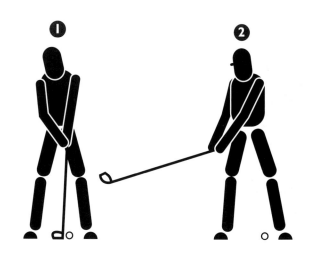

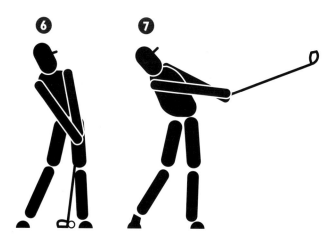

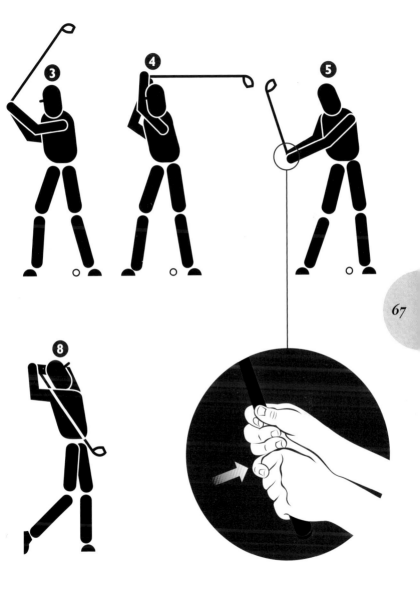

1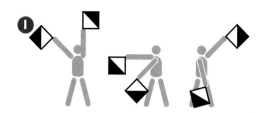

2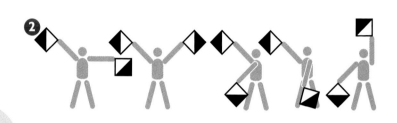

3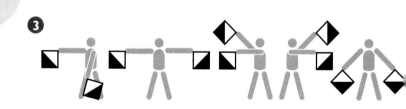

4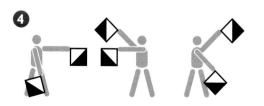

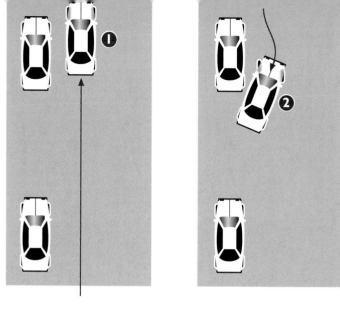

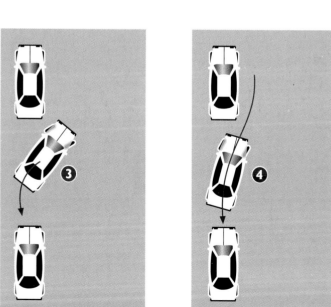

70

72

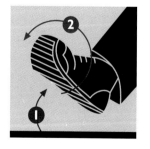

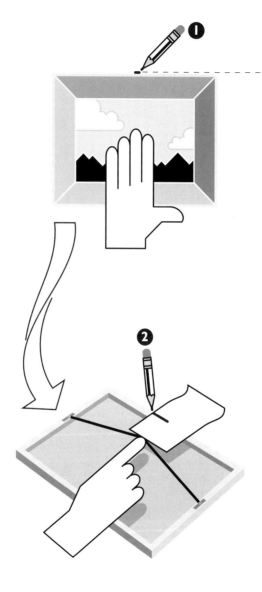

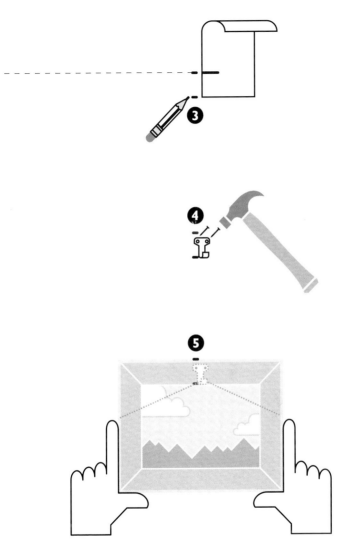

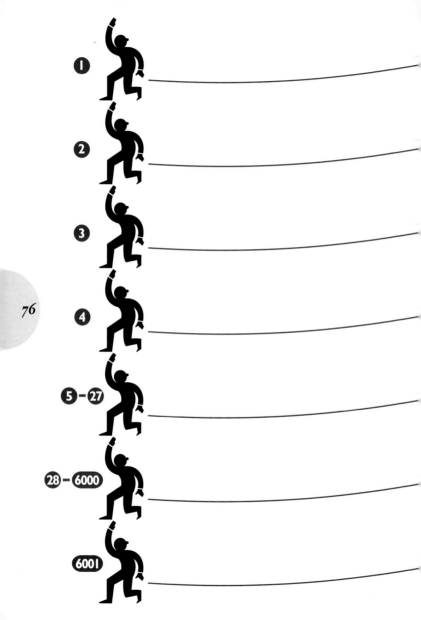

1

2

3

4

5 – **27**

28 – **6000**

6001

76

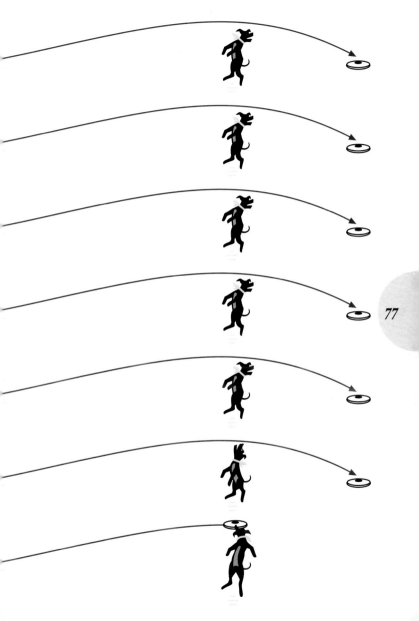

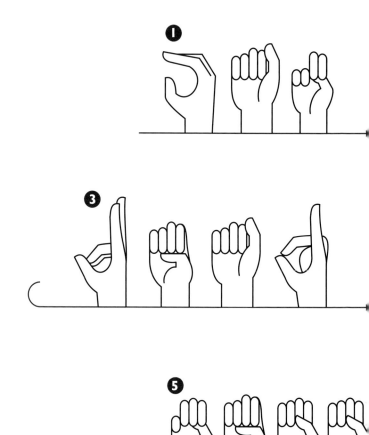

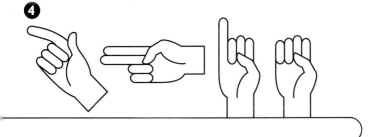

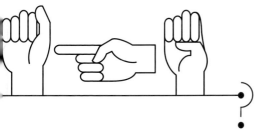

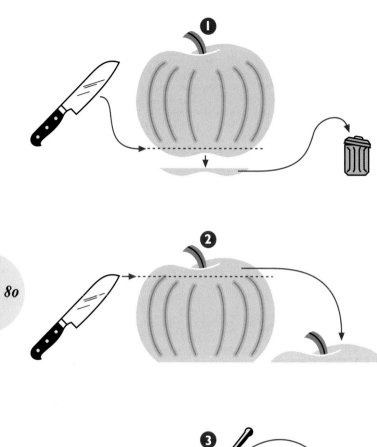

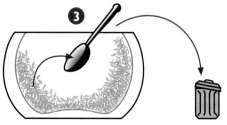

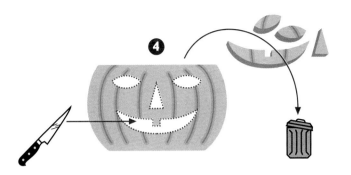

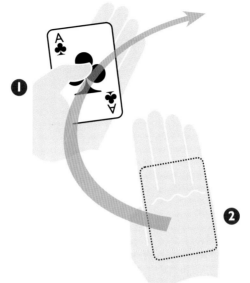

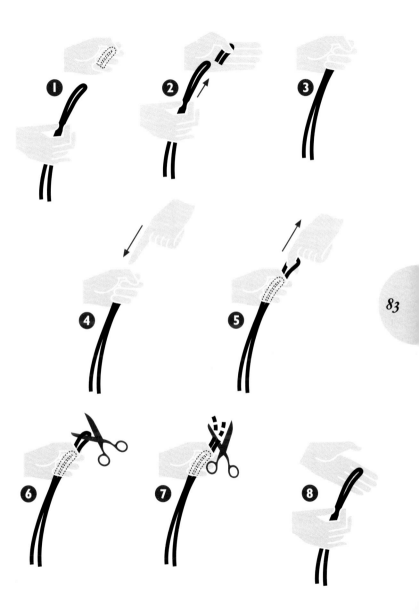

45°

1"

84

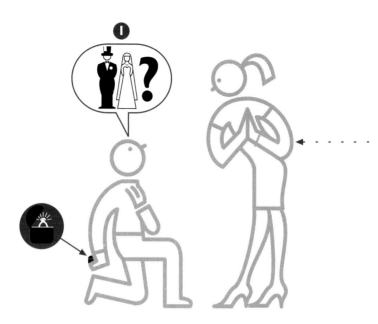

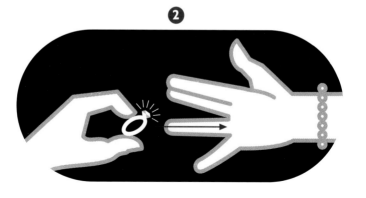

86

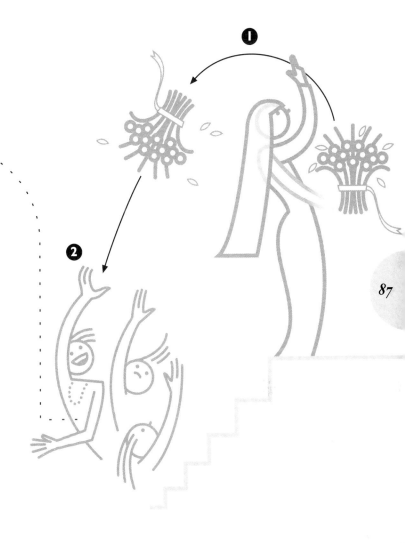

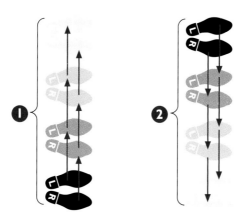

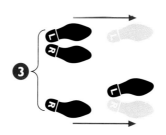

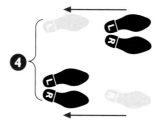

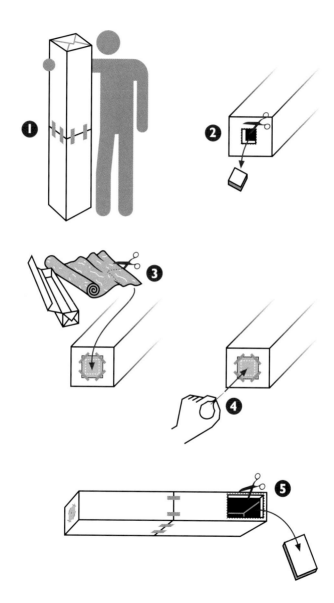

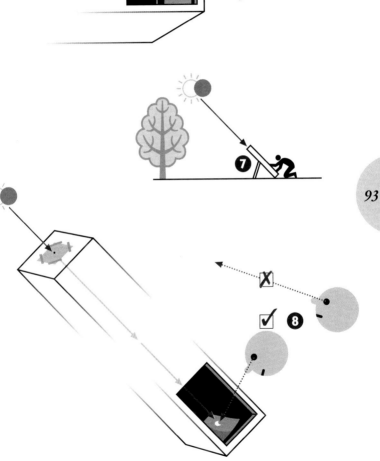

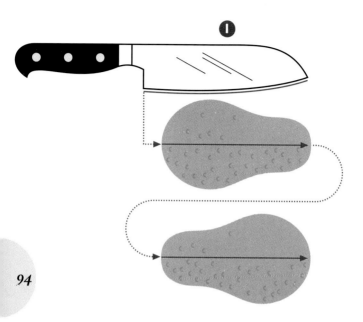

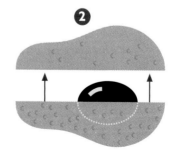

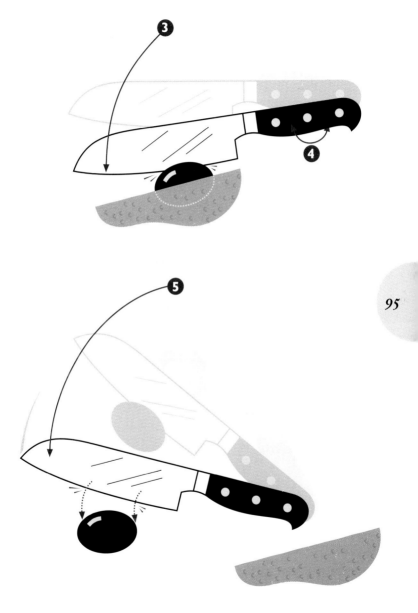

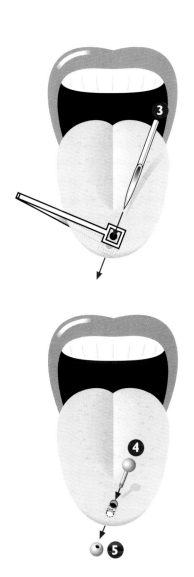

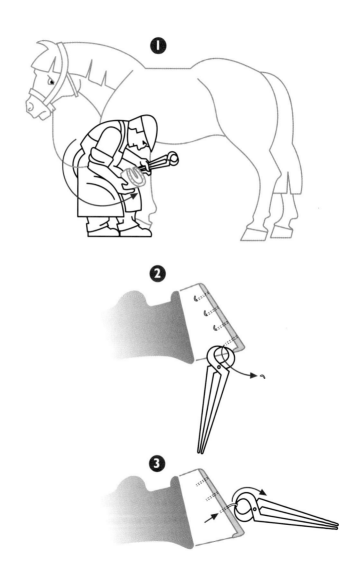

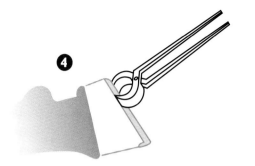

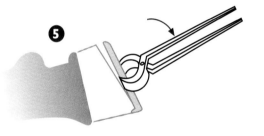

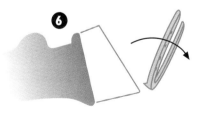

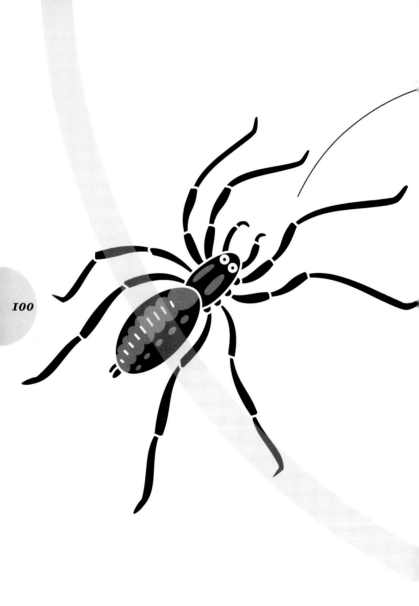

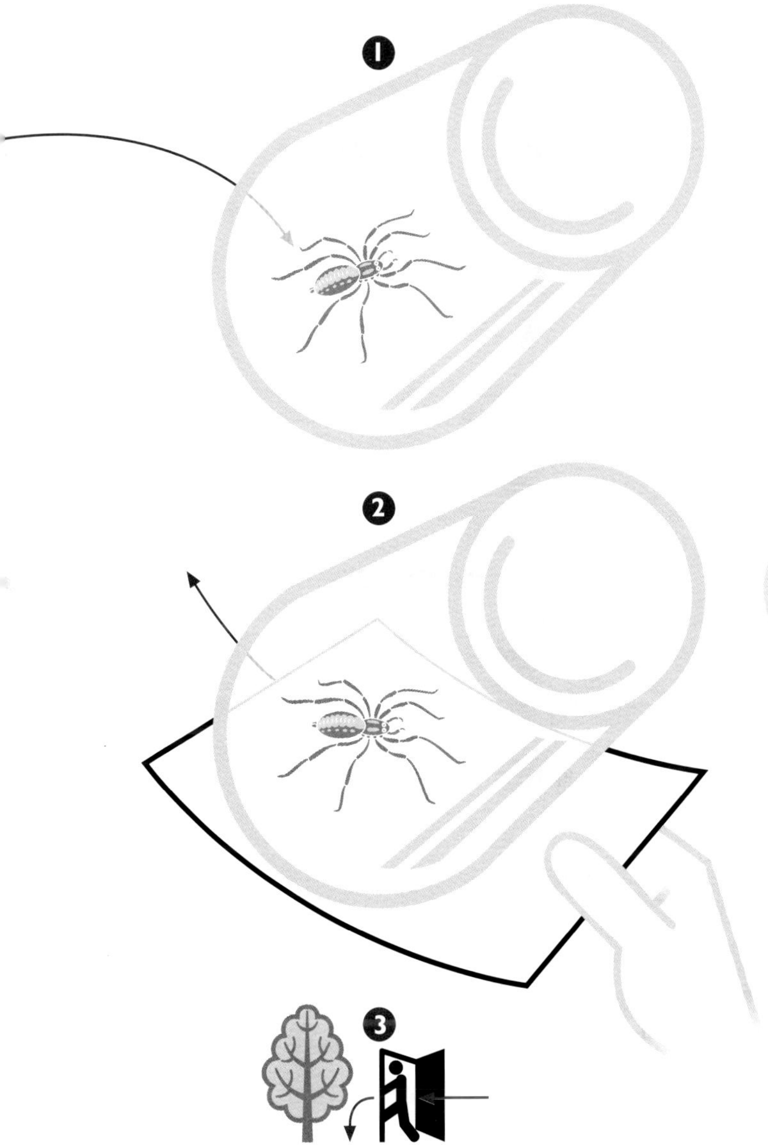
1
2
3

3

103

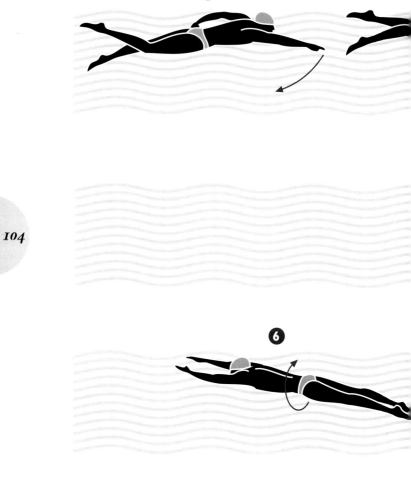

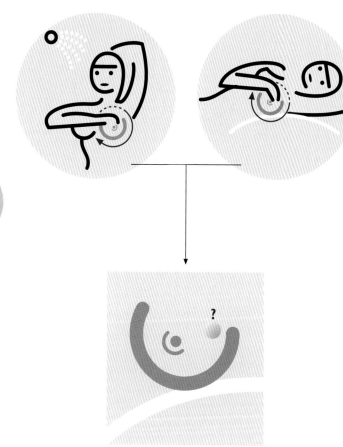

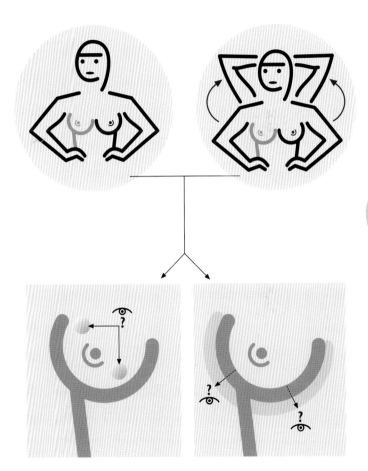

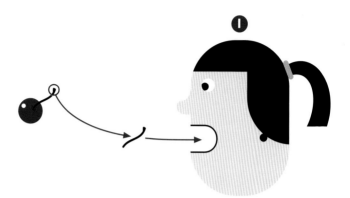

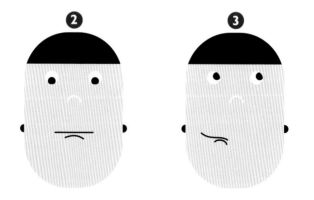

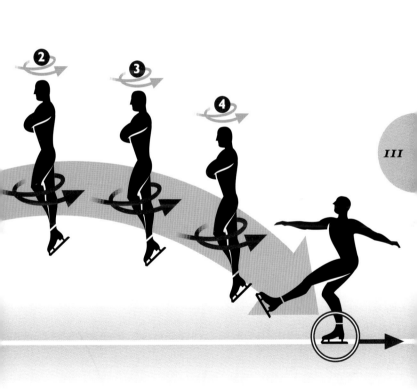

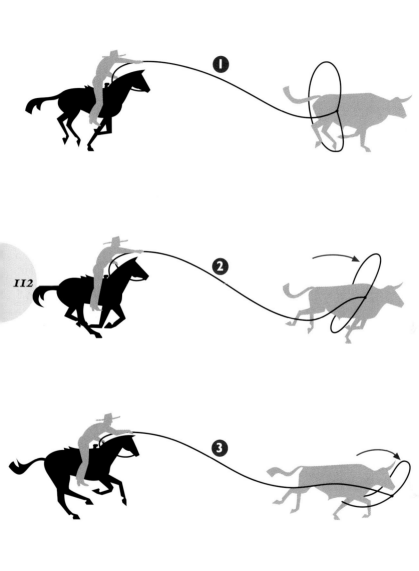

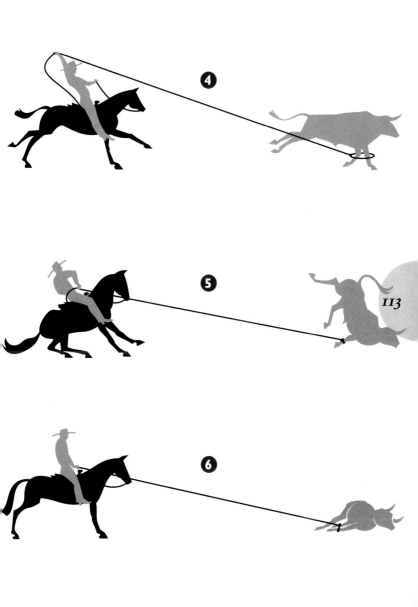

113

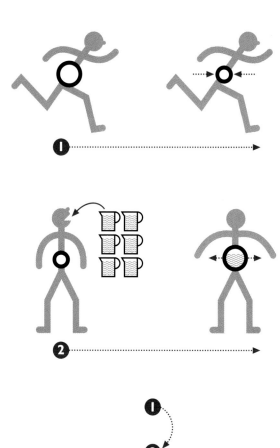

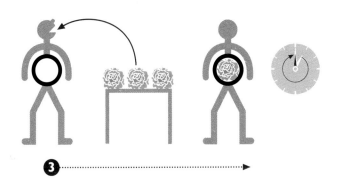

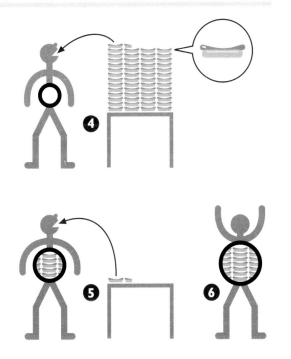

1

2

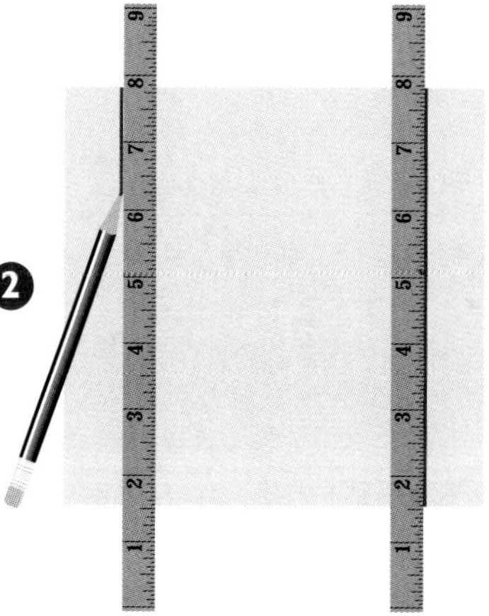

3

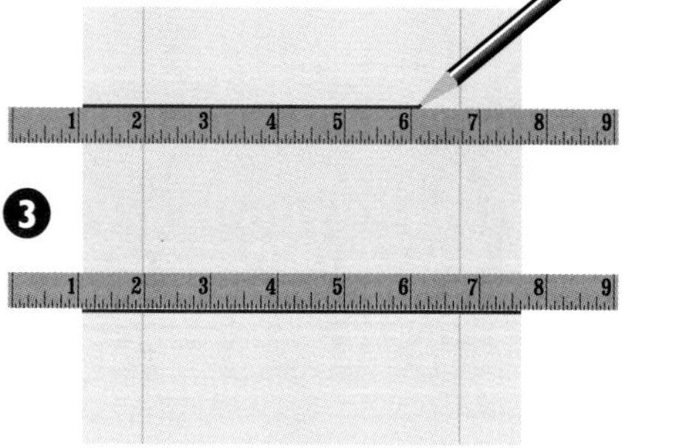

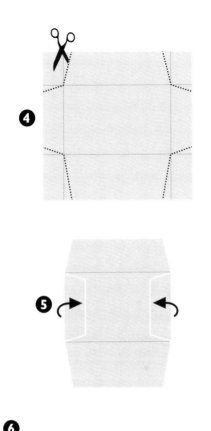

4

5

6

7

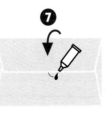

118

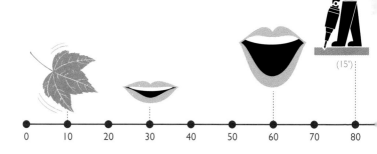

(15')

0   10   20   30   40   50   60   70   80

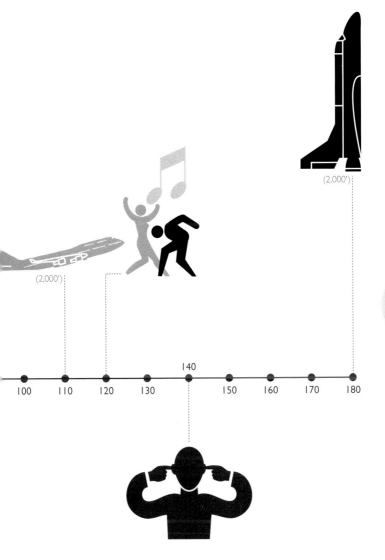

(2,000')

(2,000')

140

100   110   120   130   140   150   160   170   180

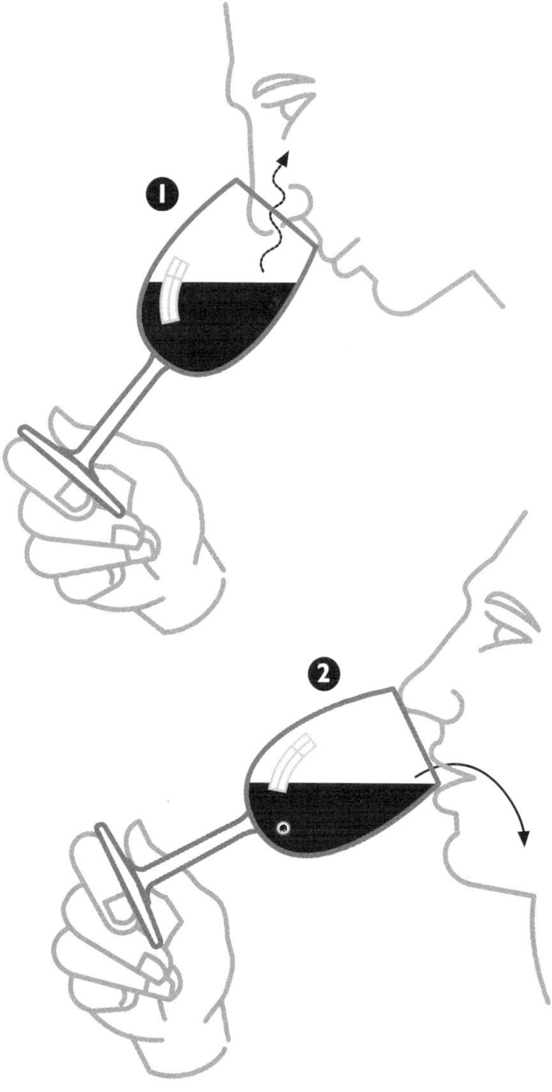
1
2

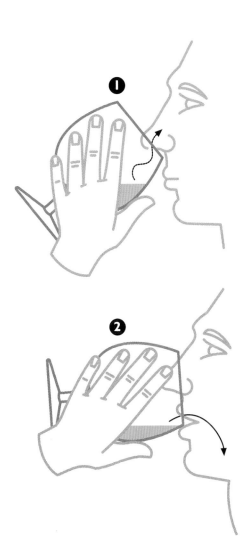

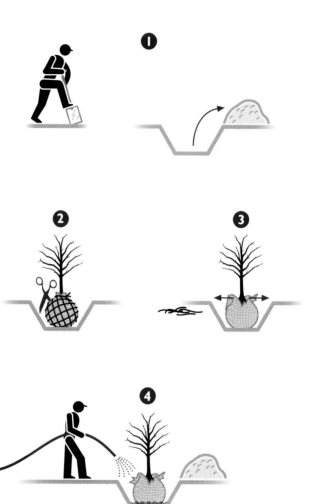

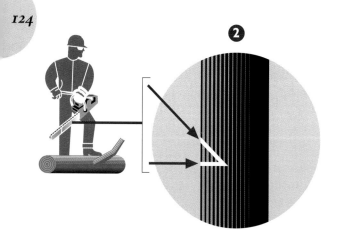

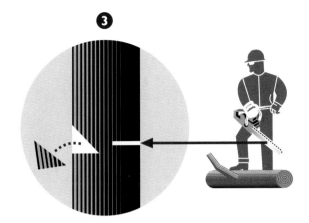

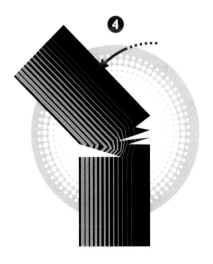

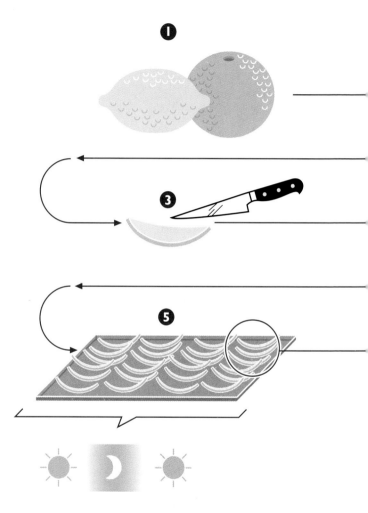

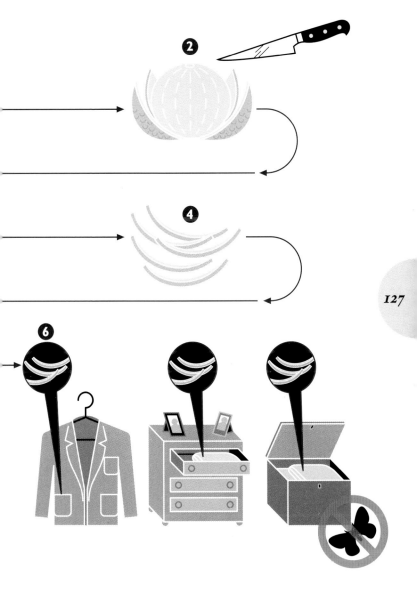

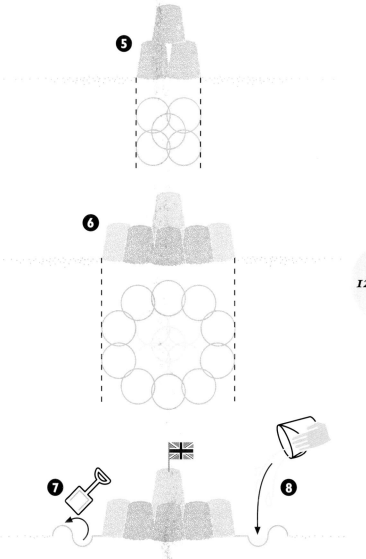

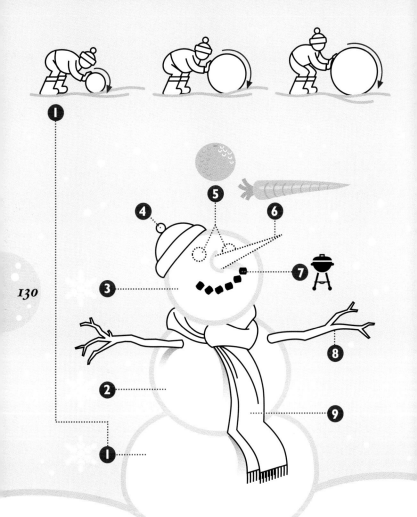

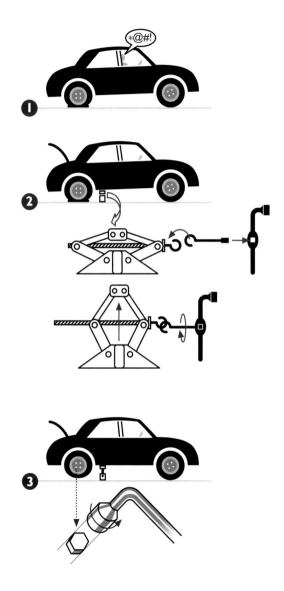

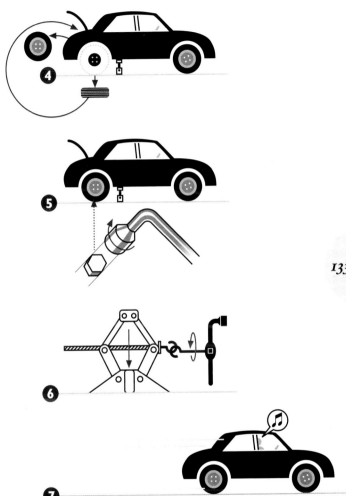

133

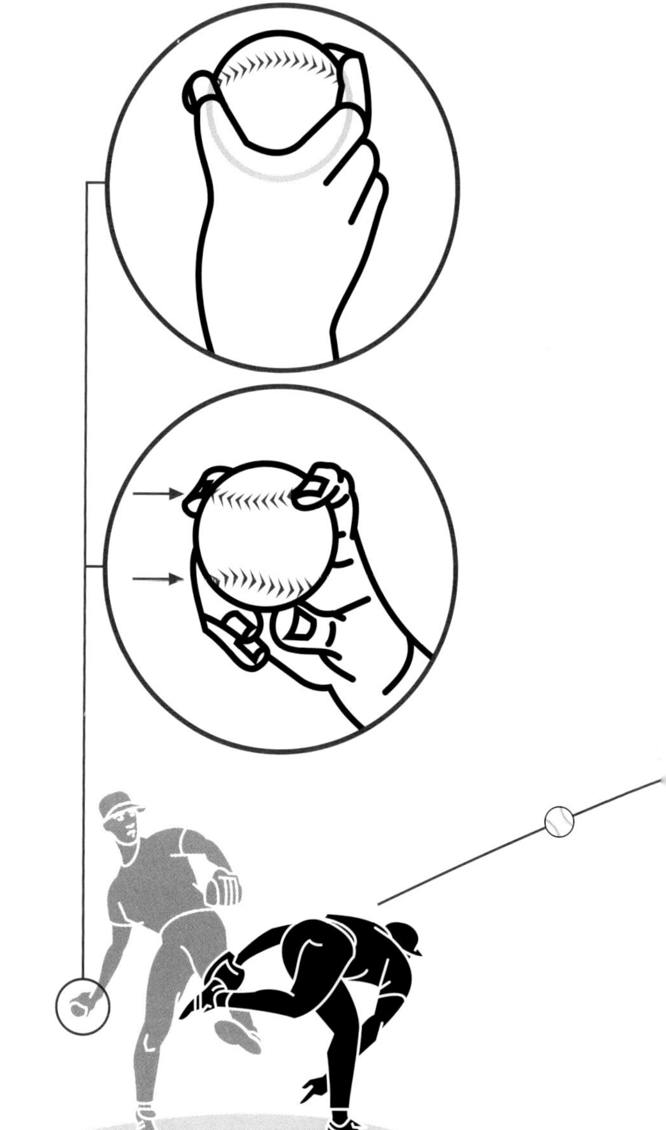

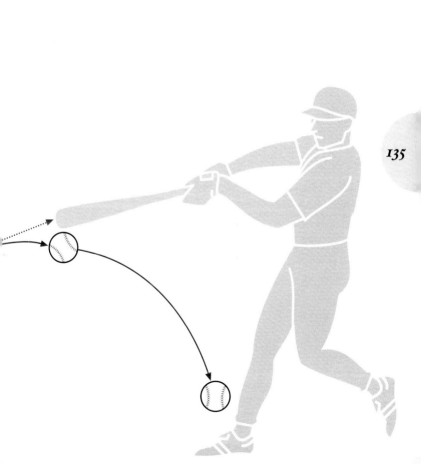

136

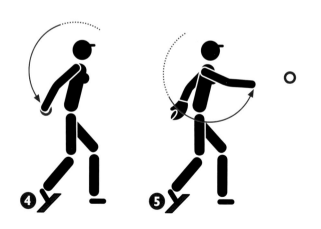

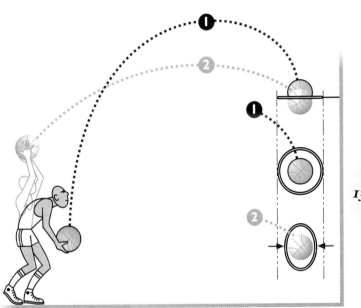

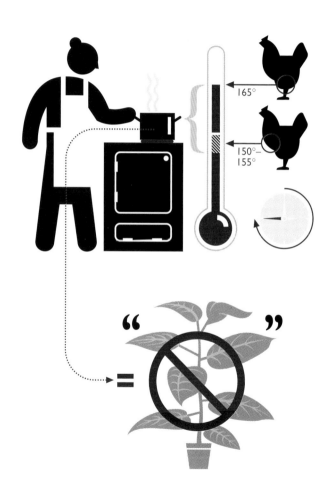

138

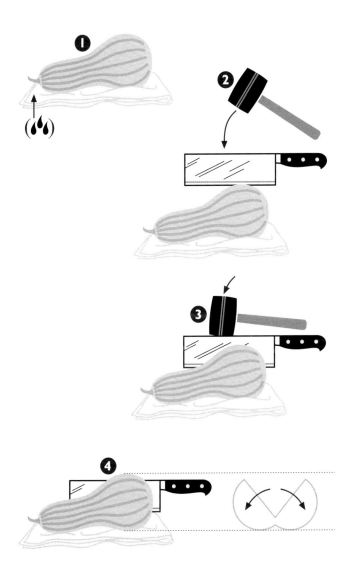

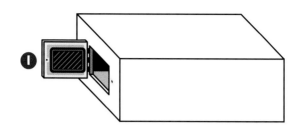

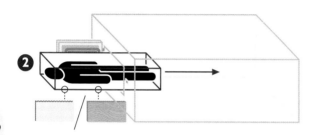

140

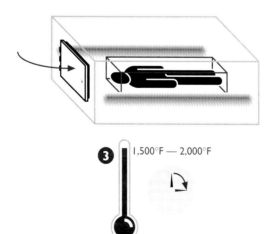

1,500°F — 2,000°F

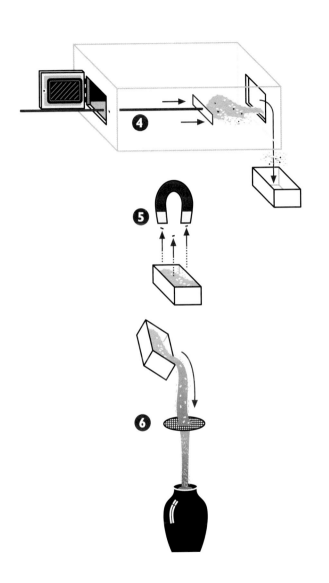

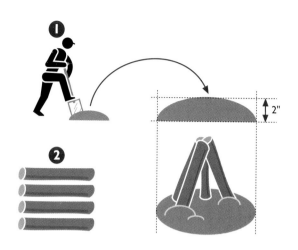

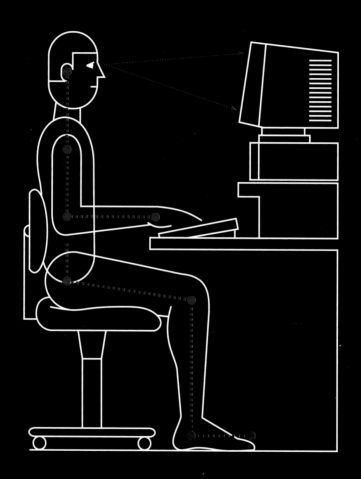

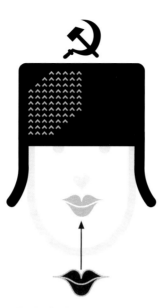

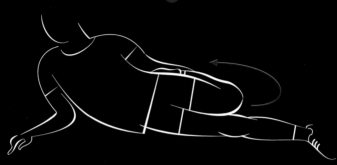

3

4

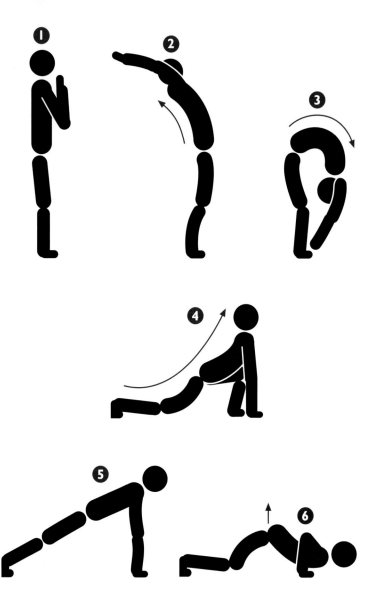

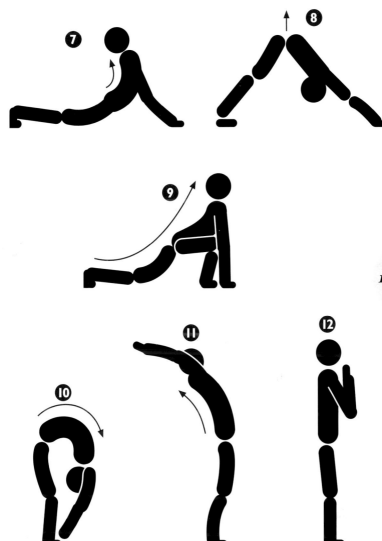

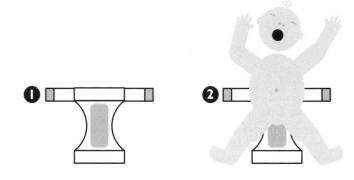

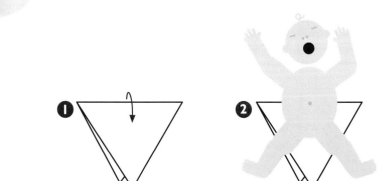

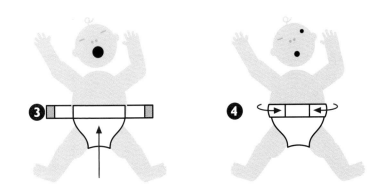

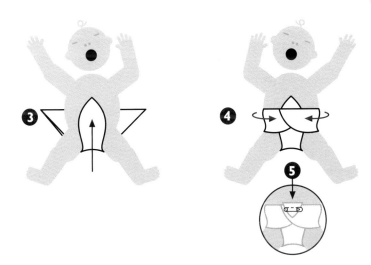

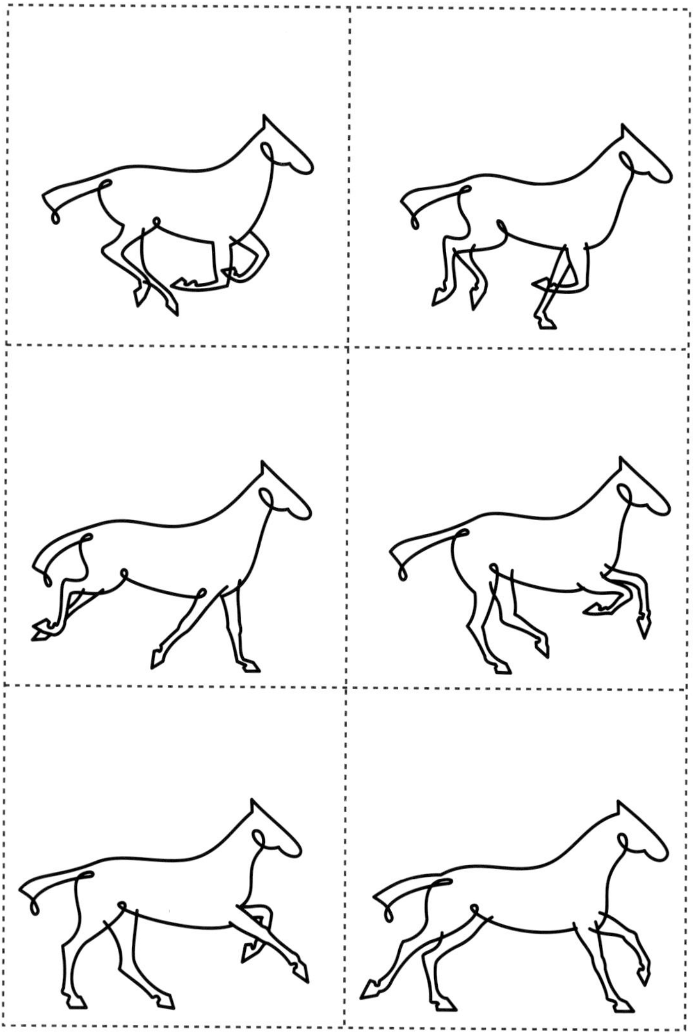

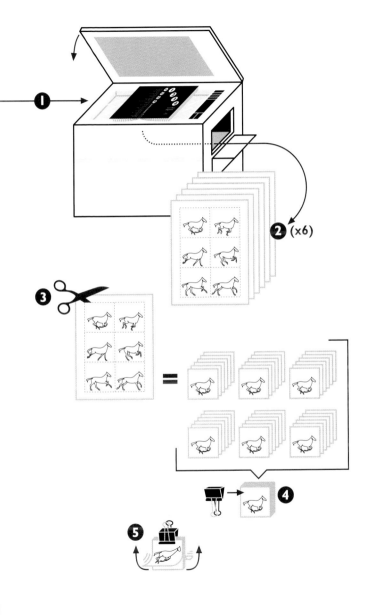

❷

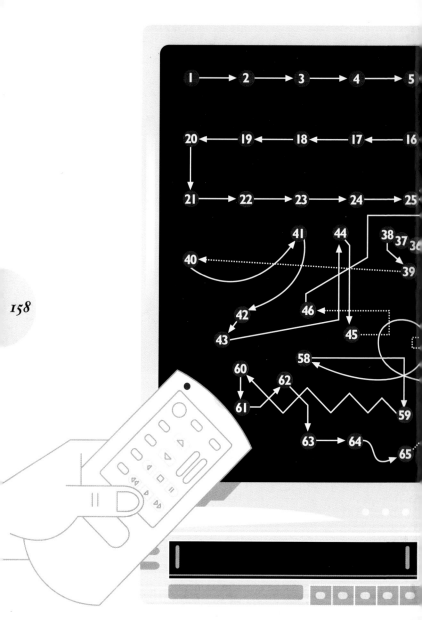

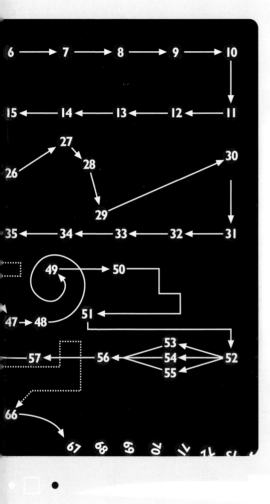

ABOUT THE ARTIST

Nigel Holmes was the graphics director of *Time* magazine, where he worked for 16 years. Before moving from England to the United States to work for *Time* in 1978, he did diagrams for the BBC and the Ford Motor Company. When he left *Time*, he started Explanation Graphics, which produces diagrams, posters, and books for a wide range of clients, from Apple and Sony to the New America Foundation and United Healthcare. His work has appeared in many magazines and newspapers, including *Discover, Esquire, Harper's, Sports Illustrated,* the *New Yorker,* and the *New York Times.* This is his fifth book.

www.nigelholmes.com